LACUNA

Laura McLauchlan

WINNIPEG: TURNSTONE PRESS, 1980

Canadian Cataloguing in Publication Data

McLauchlan, Laura
Lacuna

Poems.
ISBN 0-88801-043-5

I. Title.
PS8575.L38L3 C811'.54 C80-091057-5
PR9199.3.M32L3

ISBN 0-88801-043-5

Cover design by Brian Phillips

For Ray

Contents

Underbelly

He was somebody's father
black hair
curling up into his shorts
and down his chest
as I watched from the ground
flat breasted girl child
with hair on my head only, hair which
lurched out of twisted follicles
beneath the scalp, incipient madness
I struggled to straighten, pulling
down venetian blinds
meeting the sun's light in measured
lines precise predictable encounter
Oh Jesus, let me be
like all the others.

He was not like them.
An inland seaweed of a man
who cast his eyes down
like heavy brown nets weighted to sink
in casual violation beneath
the sun wind underbelly of birch leaves
caught half sick and longing
he drove me beyond
windows, screens, blinds
above the smoking cabins
to a high bed
of limestone where I reached
into myself and held him
like velvet in the warm
density of moss.

Autumn 1964

At dawn my father
waited with his decoys spread
the rubber ducks of man
hiding by the bullrushes to raise
a twelve-gauge voice
against birds
fly up, come on
I'll catch you, hold you
by your webbed orange feet
my hands already
smell of the marsh
where you nested last
spring, this is later

at night I swept
right to left with a flashlight
reading dirty Henry Miller and
mysteries there was a sphinx,
a Taj built for the queen
he loved to sleep with,
a wall, a Great Wall, which
kept the bones of men who
wrote, who spoke, who fought
too well for the Emperor
they went like worms
cast into mortar
flesh I thought about
skinny ingrown white
pinked at the start
swelling nipple
one of his daughters.

Alone with the stage-stuffed owls
and alabaster ladies of fortune who winked
when my ouija board spelt early
death I waited

towards sunset he'd squat on leaves
with his necklace of mallards, bluebills, pheasants
hanging above him a fading light
drew dust to pin feather as I plucked
he opened his knife.

and once more tried to teach me
to clean birds.

On Beun Retiro
for Charles

Remember the poinciana, love
I shake that flame trees long brown pod
and see our island. It is green
green and fire orange and it is
brown black bark still moist
with the essence of an Arowak girl
who lived with the sun caught
in her raised hands until
that sun fell through the casurinas
into the Caribbean years, years ago
I remember

I was your wife.

Frangipani, hibiscus,
trumpet flowers, hanging down like
triumphant bells in a festival
of vaginas, a celebration of the fecundity
of black women; white I dreamt
bleaching my skin in tubs of rust water
sweating and reading while termites made holes
in the bedroom
floor of our mansion
home of the layered white dead
the proper British dead, the now
we are living school teachers.

White men at their leisure planted
bougainvillea hedges, chenille plants,
and white women picked the plums and lemons.
All of us walked barefoot
in the garden staring down
avoiding cicadas, lizards, black widow spiders,
shuttering the house against hurricanes
while our dogs howled
death has white eyes
and carries a machete.

We were pirates together
beneath the salt water
with gold spread across us
we watched sharks, rainbow fish,
turbotte, sting rays,
while the sea kept its coral
static, sharp atrophied far beyond
flesh an excess of bone
as we moved with the liquid breeze.

Hummingbirds, sand and the scent
of jasmine at night
exiled that autumn
from northern lakes and the coming of ice
darkness came upon us like a tide.
And never had a planet seemed
so much a sun as then
when Venus lay
in that black sky
as then
when I prayed in the blue
Haitian night

Let me cease to breathe
with this man's love
still green green and fire orange
and his semen warm
between my thighs.

The First Song

Light brings knives
across our bed brings
morning slashing into the room
pushes grass through earth
pulls buds through branches
knocks the bluejay
spinning. I dress
and bring bare lips against
you feel bone and flesh
cover sleep

then I am in the backlane
walking away. Words do
return, but the first song
cuts my mouth.

At Granite Lake

I think of you
with a storm coming
the poplars restless
the loon waiting
for the moon's light
to come up
on a bird with a fish
in the moonlight.

We are not
like the moon going
to come back.
If our trouble were waning
or a season of storm
then
I'd stalk you
wild and oblivious.

But this is the ache
of earth
for her animal
when they lay
together again.

Just Outside Stratford

for Hunter MacBain

You could not take
too much sweet, diabetic
you had to watch women
who wanted to send jam
into your mouth their fresh picked
raspberries, strawberries, chokecherries
red to blue berries came too much
you couldn't take anymore

when I met you
six years as the heron flies
back large wings quiet
in the high coast of death
I come bird and once
watcher of the bird in your eyes
the feathered storm in your quiet
gnaw look I come back through
that sharp beak for the
lotus blossom other
hemisphere of mind where
we met clashing the gold light of cymbals
and laughing.

You were subtle as a mandarin,
socialist, anarchist, atheist, wealthy
businessman must be
the family black sheep
gone gray a small thin man
moored in the moon shiny light
of a huge white convertible
sailing Southern Ontario
in summer to celebrate
the ruin of Desdemona
and Lear

always mad
on the heath.

Fighting Fish

for Joy McLauchlan

There are those fish
that get away, and ones
that never fall for worms
which spin like careless flies
when men troll tiger
claws.

You know the lake
and how reeds with
every cord will
blow the iris out
this spring to turn the magii
crazy loons who want
each writhing note
to shine
the pain of labour
held like myrrh
to drive each Dowager
Empress till every marble boat
is ruined with sweat
and women hug
their flesh in nets
and webs *the nipple past*
the season
over.

You ride a ghost ship
white as opium
gray old cedar could
have danced for heads
so beautiful at thirty.

I know a woman
looks like you did then.
I'm drawn to her
she's so like you.
She comes to water
cold and dark.
She's too near ice
for men to touch.
Today at dawn I held
her deep scarred chest
and drew off hooks.

Teeth

Unbraced mouth
unbound feet
prayer book open with
witnesses interior red
brick I felt
the fatted heart of
Southern Ontario
would cast us off
flatter us foreign
bodies but the ceremony
proceeded as I smothered
laughter pulling constellations
down to the ruin
of a minister's florsheim
shoes.

Ours was a marriage
with too many teeth
they studded my jaw and
your jaw and when
our mouths met in the
you may now
kiss
the bride, she
got her
man
moment of sealing
a covenant
our teeth hit
and we drew our lips down
fast, for such days
are to pass without
teeth.

Later, as shadow boxer,
I hit you in the mouth
when I meant to
show your father how close
I could come
without striking.
Your mother gave us a mirror
to watch your swelling
lips.

You dreamt
you could write with
your thick singing
stick that wand, that gold
sax would pour honey
but your lips
caught on women's mouths
and you played seduction on
a dear friend's soft
Persian pillows. And when
my mouth held you
moving with the light
rising sun at your legs
your words came
with fear *please*
lovey, no teeth!

Winter was moaning over
our deep furnished rooms
and I held the leper's patch
to my brass monkey eyes
saw no evil compliant
as Buddha
dirt-wind-snow
was my mantra
till spring
gnawed back to nerve
howled back to sense

I left
snarling.

She Wish

Black satin rides
against her thighs
and lips are parted
under the ether of love
she wish, she wish and
she go on to a lullaby
of lace and Jesus
with his always burnin'
heart she dreamin'
and she safe.

She wish
on touching, blowing hard.
Let it be sweet,
that's all.

Tar

Truly it hurts
to leave or be left
no way of going
which hasn't a cleft
no way of leaving
which doesn't scar
and no lover gone
who hasn't been tarred.

Bubble then tar
and I'll boil up
them feathers.

Painted Territory

A poet is a reporter
who covers the beat of the dermis
and epidermis. The sinew and
flatulence of man catches his
fisherman's hook and is hauled
fresh onto the page.
Sometimes smoked, sometimes
stinking, his verse moves round
or stays like the beaver
within the painted

territory

a poetess is an eccentric
woman with a weak, flaccid heart
flabby thighs and lesbian tendencies
she is too cerebral to indulge.
She wears cotton bras, has
small withered tits and is forty
nothing. She is harmless
and will never remind you
she has genitals and is lonely.

The One About You

God but I'm tired of you men!
You strutters, you thin feathered callers
of

Luv your blue, blue eyes.
I'm fallin' in love with you
cutie pie, little round tit
charmer of me.

Listen: it's wonderful
you have a wang and I
a wong but you're wrong to believe
that wongs are consumed
with wang-envy and that because
you throw your piss further that
it is not piss at all but always
seed. Ah weep for the millions
of lives lost whenever you
can't push safely into a woman
just waiting to keep all
those lost little sperm
hoping for mother.

We ladies
your harem girls with
nursing bras
ready . . . yes, the same
sweethearts who buy garter belts
and crotchless panties to please
you, we women, have not yet
crossed you, fouled you up,
bungled your basic plan to just
fuck us and fuck us and then
to be serious, successful,
designing your buildings, researching
our breast cancer, teaching
in the university with your teddy bear
beard and your harris tweed leather bound balls.

You play with me
    Now be serious baby, come here,
    I'll lick your spikes down
    just luv you when you're angry!

Twice now you've told me
the joke about the woman who wrote
a sexy novel
An editor came all the way
from New York just to see her!

That's funny.
It means he came
for the fuck she could give him
with all that talent. *Of course*
the novel never got published.

Well, this is the one
about you.

Fruit Salad

I want more silly
talk fat words cut open
for juice, more
laugh imploded apples
can roll across this table
toss back the
oranges, grapefruits, cantaloupes
of Florida fruit sugar
brought from Safeway
in plain brown bags

I'm going to make you
fruit salad.

In the Skyline Hotel

Toronto spreads out miles east
like Gulliver tied down, and sleeping.

I am stranded eight floors up
in the Skyline Hotel watching
him in evening.

Beneath me
floors of travellers dream
while I wait, restless
as a siren

Gentle giant rise
and come quickly
to room 8122.

Vomiting the Heart

Alright, rehearse the suicide again
but not with pills, or hanging
over bridges, balconies or on
some other edge. No, wait
the time will come
just like the buyer
of the house that vacant

face, mine
in the mirror. I've
been sleeping to forget
you black bear to
snow to nothing, to itself
only

a blizzard. Good.
Perhaps I will step out
(woman off to the corner store
for bread) only
this time I'll prance
drum majorette
parading to the white apex
where I know to wait

for the cupid heart
the prairie wheat stuffed
grain-fed heart
to rise snapping the string which
holds it to its narrow
sticky cave. Ribs
break
when such an organ turns
fat loon and rises
like some eaten thing
returning to the mouth.

Lacuna

*

I sing for the lost
sheep coin chapter
the tin of soup
the one piece of meat
bit of bun the warm cup
of tea with the heart bound
tight as a pharaoh
dissolving in fits and
start tying reef knots
take stitches double
cross the rib still
hoping

the door holds
the spasm sob seizure
in this swollen closet
this cupboard where men
reach like Caesar
ransacking my chest
the chest of a diva.

I sing for Leda caught
and the carried away
Helens, the questing
Martha, the crazy Jane,
the ash-hearted Joan,
Delilah with scissors,
Persephone white
sleeping all winter

and here
women I love are sick
and so tired inside
all the old words
hang on edges
won't lay down flat
can't polish the notes
or shine up a wound
heal something
missing

**

I want the cold strawboss
who never turns over
though he pulls at the ocean
though he treats
the world as a sheet.

Abracadabra
Open Sesame
I want the moon
this is no animal
so send back
the earth's tough sinewed
cow the nursery rhyme
mama and muse
of the high jump
to the one waning tip.

***

I sing for the sun
and each day without darkness
the finder and keeper
sun loser and weeper
shrinking though vast
dwindling creation the
grower of roots and
mother of fire
the prism and rainbow
hermaphrodite worshipped
as Ra with a zillion
erections grasping for sky
and loading her hips
with pitched gold
in radiance bound
for the earth.

And I sing
for the slit, the slash,
the end of a sleep when
we rise sullen as eels
lured from our blue holes
snapping the da da god
who beats us alive
in a pulse.

Lacuna
2

I sing for this country
cool igneous crystallized
fire as sparks
ember the eye drilling
steel pins through streets
bruising her flanks
till she trusses the earth
outstripping Houdini.
With wolves she runs
north of this city.

Canada you do that.
How do you do
that disappearing act mother of
Indian, Eskimo your heart
holds a blizzard where there is
a tribe their teepees torn
open their mouths
full of beer.

You have swallowed
our ancestors
immigrants from Babylon,
Belsen, Ninevah, Brittany
mosaic you
light cutting through.
Leaving us alien
to the fifth generation.

I sing for Franklin
aground in the Arctic. For Hudson
his crew on the high sea
of mutiny. I sing
for the Argonauts of 1899
some lay with whores
all winter in Dawson
seeking the motherlode.
And mommy, oh mommy
men die reaching
you.

I sing from a temperate zone
further south through this
great gash of space
seeping over the prairie.
Northern light falling stars of
my people in this
time and place
I sing as each
cretinous sun rushes through
interstices of longing
lacuna for you.

Arcs

Like Zeus you sleep
your white arms wings
which once held down
poor Leda

It's autumn now
my fingers brush
against your hair
then fly off, dreaming
of the arcs
I'll make before
these wings turn
back to hands

and ravish you.

The Burning Bride

India, 1977

It's morning in Varanasi
bells sound light's swelling
Ganga, Ganga take down heat
swallow this wicked tongue
which Kali scrapes
across the earth through
your beating, swirling throat
she vomits and the sun rises.

And now rest my brown god
deaf mute beyond flesh
another woman walks on that
far bank. Let her red shroud
set this day's first fire.
See how she climbs
offering her arches
stepping through green
and silver anklets
as if all life had been
a dance of oleander
until her amber limbs
locked stiff.

And here is the tiger-eyed
husband of her scent
his mind deep
in one long night away
from his woman's hair.
Ganga, Ganga

Upriver boys plunge
hands first within you
turning their mouths
and coming up to sink the sky
drawing it deep beneath the murmur
of a peepal tree which brings
one shred of green
across my arm as I ride
downstream to the burning ghats

She is on fire.

Khajuraho 1

Krishna's always blue
today I set my flesh flute
in his hands and said
play white skin.
He wouldn't.
He said his lips
would drive
the tune right out
of Khajuraho shrill
into Rhajasthan where
no one knows so steep a pitch.

I've snatched the flesh
flute back for I've seen
women in the desert listen
as they sink
their brass pots
down for water.

Khajuraho 2

The trellis roots of banyan trees
take messages for earth
come into her with thanks
and live holding
held beneath root and branch
my eyes make lazy chase
on monkeys playing overhead.

Twenty steps beyond me
the temple is red ash
but she, this one
stone woman, stands.
Four lovers bend
to suck her melons
their orchid tongues
ring tiny bells strung
cross her buttocks
moving down and up
the sphincter their hands
catch where

she keeps them.

Doctor Bethune

for Phyllis and Jessie Berck

You saved lives
evangelist seeker of salvation
in the flesh. Tubercular
you invented shears
to snap a ribcage open
and collapse the sinking
lung *just to breathe air!*

Death was your sweet blond
angel when you painted
"T.B.'s Progress" she
pushed your brush like feet
climbing up to dance
the date of coming death
upon that canvas was your
headstone where it was written
she'd be back October
1927 when you'd finally settled
things with Francis.
But you never would
though for twelve years more
you travelled mostly
letting go it was all
thread unwinding deep between
her arms sometimes that
loving drove you mad. You
were past surgeons long before
you cut yourself and died.

Always it was the ripped
men you could sew up
you the surgeon cut to the brain
could stitch the wounds
which bled and could be closed.
But otherwise you were a wolf
who waited for fools and set on them
snarling: too rich, wealthy
Westmount's gray old money
made you nauseous, loud,
drunk, and bitter at the crushed velvet
parties they held themselves
up to the light like crystal
you wanted to smash — for nothing
budged — you joined the Communists
dreaming fat would be lean, and lean
would not stay hungry.

You broke away from Montreal,
Sacre Coeur and Canada
to fight Franco
with the transfused blood
of women and men who lined up
before sunrise on the streets of Madrid
waiting for your needle to take
blood to their brothers, the husbands,
the fathers, the sons fighting the fascists.

In 1937 you went to China
to find the Eighth Route Army
in Yenan you met with Mao-Tse-Tung
late in the cave of China's hope
searching for that most vital part
was blood in the nineteen months you worked
eighteen hour day-to-night
live wire no other man could touch.
So lonely in your sleep — the little sleep
you had — few letters reached
into the night you typed your friend Barnwell
a letter *Books — are books still being written?*
Is music still being played?
Do women still love to be loved?

Then septicaemia attacked
and you who had saved so many had
no drug or man to save yourself
the sum of your blood-poisoned parts
died while all those round you
wept. Yes, women still love
to be loved.

Opening

On this worn carpet
cast off shed as a skin
I claim my cross-legged self
apex of opening
split delta celebrant
of that soft dark mine
and my light skin waiting
on flowers of wool.

Flesh bee in the it of it
the She and the He of it
between stamen and pistil
buzzing the pit of a skin.

Ancestors

They are under the earth
and in towers of silence
where vultures come and stay
down till the bones drop
they keep in fine linen
the cat gut thread of the royal
brain curling asleep.

They lie like Mumtaz
with her shah in mausoleums
inlaid with sapphire and in
tholos tombs with high lintels
beneath doors robbers tunnel
like gophers to take
the white jade
from their lips.

Each has a niche
a last perch
in the family tree
we fall heir
to the passing of breath
drawn up as genii
spent in oily summers
taken held
and let go.

*

Old woman
covers herself with
moon and water
when I'd cipher
the brail from
her heart.

**

She waits
like a sepia ikon
in my dusty hall.
She is the sleek girl
with starch thick under lace
her breasts moulded to wire
her flesh foiled
in silk
her ribbons go miles
back to a man
far from the lens
and my eyes on her
soft full face
drawn from mother's
mother's mother
madonna

Nothin' special
but her tea scones
were ivory.

He was a tall man
gray in Bombay's heat
her sailor
before the rains
chained him like a dwarf
tucking limbs down to
fever's long red hull.
She called like
a mermaid till he came
and fell cross the bed.

The heather was scarlet
last autumn where
you threw love's first
million seeds
and now I've a child
to raise with the waves

and she'll play
on the floors of the sea.

Years followed her
locking, sealing, stopping
with his pulse
rubbing her youth
like a thing lost to pumice.

Wife is silk
and widow rag
washing over and over
mother of once
and sweet Jesus again
turning back where
goose feather quilts
weighed like fresh peat
cut from the highland of sleep
and forget wanting to hold
as women want only
the keeping of babes
in the steel arms of a ship
she rocked to the new world
from Glasgow to Montreal
where she caught her
train to Winnipeg, descending
a thin-lipped old woman
ready
to stake bones
in the earth.

***

The daughters of kelp
and salt water call
from the reefs with the stars
round their bellies
and I am with them
tonight beside you
rise and spit
rise and spit.
Breathe like a runner
dance an hour
in my arms though white
the descendant of Zulus.
Give a yelp
for the skull and the scalp
and all the live wire
which you hurl
within me

the maybe
when we take chances.

"Close that door which
is ajar in the entrails
of that mirror." "This one?" "No; its sister."

"It cannot be closed. One can
never arrive at that place
where the door-latches act unbound.

Such is the spot that I am sure of..

"Trilce"
Cesar Vallejo: The Complete Posthumous Poetry
trans. Clayton Eshleman & Jose Rubia Barcia
(Berkeley: University of California Press., 1978)

Turnstone Press
Lacuna
by Laura McLauchlan

Turnstone Press gratefully acknowledges grants from the Manitoba Arts Council and the Canada Council which have aided in the publication of this book.

Turnstone Press
St. John's College
University of Manitoba
Winnipeg, Manitoba
R3T 2M5

Books by Turnstone Press

In the Gutting Shed by W.D. Valgardson
Open Country by George Amabile
the lands I am by Patrick Friesen
Changehouse by Michael Tregebov
Seems Valuable by Ed Upward
Seed Catalogue by Robert Kroetsch
The Inside Animal by Arthur Adamson
Blowing Dust off the Lens by Jim Wallace
bluebottle by Patrick Friesen
Soviet Poems by Ralph Gustafson
Rehearsal for Dancers by Craig Powell
Mister Never by Miriam Waddington
The Cranberry Tree by Enid Delgatty Rutland
Rock Painter by R.E. Rashley
First Ghost to Canada by Kenneth McRobbie
No Longer Two People by Patrick Lane and Lorna Uher
The Earth Is One Body by David Waltner-Toews
The Man with the Styrofoam Head by Gregory Grace
When the Dogs Bark at Night by Valerie Reed
The Bridge, That Summer by A.E. Ammeter
This Body That I Live In by Anne Le Dressay
Mother's Gone Fishing by Norma Dillon
Almost a Ritual by Les Siemieniuk
Jimmy Bang Poems by Victor Enns
Across the White Lawn by Robert Foster
Shore Lines by Douglas Barbour
No Country for White Men by Gordon Turner
Interstices of Night by Terrence Heath
A Planet Mostly Sea by Tom Wayman
Scarecrow by Douglas Smith
Leaving by Dennis Cooley
The Light of Our Bones by Douglas Smith
Settlement Poems 1 by Kristjana Gunnars
I Want to Tell You Lies by John Lane
Humans and Other Beasts by Lorna Uher
Marsh Burning by David Arnason